HOMEMADE VINEGAR

made with

MOTHER OF VINEGAR

HOMEMADE VINEGAR

made with

MOTHER OF VINEGAR

Easy to make

with complete instructions

Patrick Burke Watkins
with
Carole Carla Watkins

First Edition

A - Publishing, Napa, California

HOMEMADE VINEGAR

MADE WITH

MOTHER OF VINEGAR

Published by:

A - Publishing
Post Office Box 5523
Napa, CA 94581 U. S. A.

Copyright 1995, by Patrick B. Watkins
and Carole C Watkins

First Printing 1995

Printed in the United States of America
ISBN   0-9630941-4-0   Softcover

ABOUT THE AUTHOR & AUTHORESS

Pat and Carole have been affiliated with the home wine and beermaking trade for over ten years. They enjoy do it yourself projects and having made their own homemade wine and beer; it seemed to follow that making homemade vinegar would be interesting. It was, and is. Although when they began making homemade vinegar there seemed to be little available published information on the scope of the subject, they were determined that they could make great palatable homemade vinegar.

As a result, through research and during the process of making numerous batches of home-made vinegar, that they shared with family and friends. They came up with a considerable amount of practical information that can be used to produce excellent homemade vinegar.

DISCLAIMER

The purpose of this book is to enlighten and entertain and the contents are for information only. Therefore the information should only be used as a general guide and not the conclusive source of vinegar making information. Neither the authors nor the publisher assumes any responsibility for the use or misuse of information contained in this book.

DISCLAIMER

TABLE OF CONTENTS

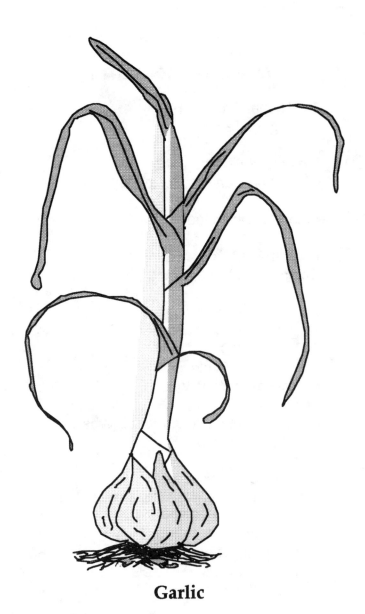

Garlic

Add herbs to your homemade vinegar

TRADITIONAL PROCEDURE

This is the procedure for making your own homemade vinegar with acetobacter, commonly known as <u>mother of vinegar</u>, and herein often referred to as <u>mother</u>. We hope you will read the entire book before making your first batch of vinegar. It contains a great deal of information that can be useful when making fine homemade wine vinegar. <u>Especially read the chapters on</u> **Mother, Water and Wine,** and **Clean and Sanitize Everything.**

Makings of vinegar:

The proper **amounts** of <u>mother of vinegar</u>, <u>water</u>, and <u>wine</u> and a sufficient amount of <u>air</u> are important when starting your vinegar. They will help the batch convert in less time and produce better vinegar.

Measure the amount of <u>mother of vinegar</u>, water and wine you will need.

ONE PART MOTHER OF VINEGAR

ONE PART WATER (If your water contains chlorine, draw off the amount you are going to use. Let it set, covered with a clean sanitized cloth overnight before you use it. If your water does not contain chlorine, boil and let it cool before using.)

TWO PARTS DRY WINE, 11% to 12% alcohol

(**Example**- -<u>one pint</u> mother of vinegar, <u>one pint</u> water, and <u>two pints</u> wine.) When starting your vinegar with wine that has 11% to 12% alcohol, these amounts are important and should be followed closely. Reduce the amount of water if the wine you use contains less alcohol.

<u>Example</u>
Wine with 9% alcohol, use
<u>one pint</u> mother of vinegar,
<u>one quarter pint</u> water, and
<u>two and 3/4 pints</u> wine.

Wine, and apple cider with 6% alcohol, use <u>one pint</u> mother of vinegar, <u>no water,</u> and <u>three pints</u> wine.

Container: If you have less than a half pint of mother, you can start your first batch of vinegar in a **quart** canning jar. If you have a pint or more of mother, you can start it in a **one gallon**, <u>widemouth</u> glass jar or a <u>widemouth</u> food grade plastic container (preferably with a spigot that can be removed for cleaning).

Measure the amount of mother, water and wine you are going to need; pour the **wine and water** into a clean, sanitized, widemouth glass jar or plastic container. **Shake or stir vigorously,** and let it set for about **30 minutes** before you **add the mother.**   This amount of time will allow some of the sulfite gas (potassium metabisulfite or sodium bisulfite) in the wine to escape.

Now, pour the mother of vinegar into the container of water and wine and gently stir. Leave a **couple of inches** of space in the top of the container as the mixture needs air to breathe. If the mixture fills the container, pour the surplus into a smaller container.

Cover the top of the container(s) with a clean, sanitized, tight wove cloth, such as a piece of white muslin (sheet material) or several layers of cheesecloth. You can use a large rubber band to keep the cover in place, or tie the cover securely to the top of the container. A cloth or cheesecloth cover <u>will allow the mixture to breathe</u> as it needs as much air as possible while converting to vinegar. The cover will also help keep dust and insects out of your potential vinegar.

Storing: The container of mother, water and wine **should be stored** in an area that is not **too hot** nor **too cold.** If the temperature where it is stored is too hot, above 90 degrees, the heat can seriously impair the mother; if too cold, below 65 degrees, the mother will slow down and may stop working. The mixture will convert to vinegar sooner if the temperature where it is stored is between **70** and **80** degrees F. Having a thermometer in the same area where you store it helps you keep track of the temperature. Store the container of potential vinegar where there is no direct sunlight, preferably in a **fairly dark** area and away from any **drafts** where the temperature can fluctuate suddenly.

In a week or so, a gelatinous cap, <u>layer of mother</u> should begin to form on the top of your potential vinegar. It will grow and cover the entire top of mixture, and as time goes by it will become thicker and more solid. The cap can have a grayish or brownish color and as it grows it may look a little like soft wet chamois leather.

Recap:

1. Use a widemouth glass jar or food grade plastic container, large enough to have about two inches of air space between the top of the liquid and the top of the bottle.

2. Draw off amount of water required, let it set overnight, or boil it, and let cool.

3. Add wine to water, shake or stir vigorously, let set for 30 minutes.

4. Add mother of vinegar.

5. Cover the container with a sanitized cloth.

6. Store the container of potential vinegar in an area away from direct sunlight and

drafts, and preferably where the temperature of the area stays between 70 and 80 degrees F.

Things to watch and smell: Mold appearing on the top of the vinegar, a musty odor, smells somewhat like lacquer thinner, or smells other than the aroma of vinegar. If any of these develop, get rid of the batch, sanitize the container and start a new batch of vinegar, but before you do, refer to:

Sanitary conditions: Did you wash, sanitize and rinse everything that contacted the liquid mixture?

Procedure: Did you use the right amounts of mother, water and wine?

Water: If your water contains chlorine, did you draw it off in a sanitized container and let it set covered overnight to allow some of the chlorine to escape? If your water does not contain chlorine, did you boil the water to kill any bacteria that might be in it? (See page 21)

Wine: Did the wine you used have an offensive odor, unpleasant or sour taste? (See page 23)

TESTING FOR TASTE

In a few weeks to three months, plus or minus, according to the conditions where it is stored (heat, cold, light or dark), a good solid cap (layer of mother) should have formed on the top of the batch. The conversion from mother, water and wine to vinegar should be complete.

If your container has a spigot, draw off a tablespoon full of vinegar for testing. If your container does not have a spigot, remove the layer of mother on top of the vinegar, discard it, and dip out a tablespoon full of vinegar. If the layer of mother sinks to the bottom of the container when you try to remove it, don't worry. You can remove the layer that sank when you clean out the container to start a new batch. The new batch will grow another layer of mother.

Testing:

This is the method we use for testing to see if the mixture has converted to the vinegar taste we like. Place a sugar cube in the tablespoon of vinegar for a few seconds then take it out and suck or chew the sugar cube. If you cannot use sugar for whatever reason, have someone test it for you. At first the sweet taste of the sugar will be dominant, but you will learn to ignore the sweetness after you test your vinegar a few times. Testing this way should give you the flavor of the vinegar, and should to tell you if it is too weak, just right, or too strong.

If the vinegar taste and flavors are **too weak**, let the mixture work another week or so and test it again. If it is **just right**, use it. If the vinegar taste is **too strong**, draw off the amount you are going to use and dilute it with water. Be careful when adding water. Just add a little water, then test it again. Repeat until you get the strength you want.

When the vinegar is finished to your satisfaction, draw off the amount you want in a glass jar or bottle and cap with a plastic lid. It is ready to use and can be stored in a refrigerator, where it will remain dormant.

Be sure to **leave some vinegar** in the container. The vinegar you leave is **mother of vinegar**. Measure the amount you leave; add more water and wine to a clean, sanitized, rinsed container in the same proportion as in <u>procedure</u>, stir and let it set for about thirty minutes, <u>then add the mother</u>. In a short time, a layer of mother will begin to form on the top, and you are on your way to making another batch of fine vinegar.

You can also pour the remaining <u>vinegar</u> into a clean, sanitized, rinsed jar or bottle and secure with a plastic cap. (Use a jar or bottle that you can fill to the top with the vinegar, and store the container in a cupboard.) Without air, the mother will remain dormant until you are ready to make another batch of vinegar.

Don't wait too long to make your next batch, as you may use up the amount you made and have to wait until the new batch is ready.

NOTES ON PROCEDURE AND TESTING FOR TASTE

MOTHER, WATER AND WINE

Mother of vinegar:

A vinegar culture, generally known as <u>mother of vinegar</u>, is a culture that forms a cap or layer of mother on the top of the potential vinegar. It is an interesting process to watch as conversion from the ingredients (mother, water and wine) to vinegar takes place.

Mother of vinegar can be obtained in a red culture for red wine and a white culture for white wine. It is best to start a <u>red wine vinegar with red mother of vinegar</u>, and a <u>white wine vinegar with white mother of vinegar</u>. Although, let's say you want to make a red wine vinegar, and for whatever reason you cannot locate any red mother of vinegar, you can start your vinegar with

19

white mother of vinegar, water, and a red wine. The batch will be much lighter in color than the red wine, but when the batch converts to vinegar and you add more water and red wine to make more vinegar, the dominate red color and flavor of the red wine will increase.

If you have red mother of vinegar and you want to make a white vinegar with white wine, the opposite will occur. Your batch will start with a pale red or pinkish color, but when it converts to vinegar and you add more water and white wine, to make more vinegar, the color will gradually clear and the flavor of the white wine will increase.

Regardless of which mother you use, a red or white, for eventual full flavor and aroma it is best to stay with the kind of wine you start with. For example, if you start your vinegar with a burgundy wine, only add burgundy wine to your vinegar as you increase the amount of vinegar you are making.

Water:

Too much chlorine in the water you use when making your vinegar, can destroy the mother of vinegar. If your water contains chlorine and you think it may cause a problem, draw off the amount of water you need in a clean, sanitized and rinsed container before you start your vinegar. Let the water sit, covered with a clean, sanitized cloth for 24 hours. This will allow some of the chlorine gas in the water to escape and reduce the amount of chlorine in the water. If you choose, you can boil the water to reduce the amount of chlorine. If you boil the water, allow it to cool to 70 - 75 degrees F. before you mix it with the wine and mother.

If your water source does not contain chlorine, it may be advisable to boil it anyway. The water may contain a bacterium you are not aware of, that could affect the outcome of your batch of vinegar.

Water that has a high content of iron and or sulfur can affect finished vinegar, as iron and or sulfur residue can create iron haze and or unpleasant odors in your vinegar. If your water contains a high percentage of these or other minerals you may want to get the water for your vinegar from another source. Most regular commercially bottled drinking water may be used without treating.

NOTES ON WATER USED

Source of your water, city water, well water, commercially bottled water. Did you treat your water, if so how?

Wine:

Do not listen to the old tale; that vinegar can be made with wine regardless of how bad the wine tastes or smells--although to some extent it is true. <u>Make your vinegar with a good wine;</u> or your chance of making a pleasing, palatable, homemade vinegar is very slim, almost non existent.

If the wine you are going to use has an unpleasant odor, smells musty, or does not taste as it should, the wine should not be used for making vinegar. The finished vinegar could have a disagreeable taste, and or offensive odor of the wine. Be particular about the wine you use when making your vinegar. We always open a new bottle or jug of wine and pour a wee sample for taste and aroma. If it smells and tastes as good as we think it should, we use it when making our vinegar. If it doesn't, we do not use it for vinegar.

Again, when adding wine to your <u>working vinegar,</u> for the full flavor and aroma a particular wine gives vinegar, stay with the kind of wine you started with. Example, if you start your vinegar with burgundy wine, only add burgundy wine to your vinegar.

Belated thought: If you happen to have a bottle of <u>recorked</u> wine, of the same kind you are making your vinegar with (example, Zinfandel) left over from the night before (slim chance) and the wine still tastes good. You might add the proper amount of water to it and pour it into your batch of working vinegar.

You can also ignore the ground rule and pour any kind of wine you may have leftover from a party or whatever, into your vinegar. However, if you do, there is no guarantee as to the flavor and aroma your vinegar will end up with. As someone said, "to each his own." You may think the finished vinegar is great, or you may not. If you make this kind of vinegar, we would suggest you make it as a separate experimental batch, other than your regular vinegar.

When using wine with 11% or 12% alcohol, do not over wine your vinegar! When adding more wine to your vinegar, stay with the proportions recommended, (<u>one part vinegar, one part water</u> and <u>two parts wine)</u>. If you add only wine and no water, the alcohol content may get too high in the vinegar and destroy the mother.

24

CLEAN AND SANITIZE
EQUIPMENT, ETC.

We definitely believe that most failures in making homemade vinegar (and wine and beer for that matter) are due to lack of cleanliness and sanitizing. When making your vinegar, it is very important to keep your hands, measuring cups, containers, cover material and any other equipment you use, clean and sanitized, to avoid contaminating the vinegar. Remember this is a food product you are working with. You, your family and friends are going to consume it.

Tri Sodium Phosphate (TSP) is a good equipment cleaner. Chlorinated Tri Sodium Phosphate is a cleaner and sanitizer. After cleaning, rinse the equipment with water, then unless you used Chlorinated Tri Sodium

Phosphate, rinse everything with a sanitizing solution and again rinse everything with clean water. If you do not rinse off most cleaning and sanitizing solutions, they can create an unpleasant taste in your vinegar and if too strong can destroy the mother of vinegar. Soap or detergents are not recommended for cleaning as they can leave a film or residue on the equipment and bottles, which may also leave a taste in your vinegar. Failures, when making homemade vinegar, wine or beer as we said, are often due to not keeping everything clean, sanitized and rinsed.

Sanitizing Solutions:

A sanitizer that has worked well for us for sanitizing equipment, containers, bottles, etc., when we make homemade vinegar, wine or beer is a product called B-T-F Iodine. Its liquid form makes it extremely convenient to use, and its color when mixed with water, makes it easy to judge the quantities to use. If you can see any color when you mix it with water, you've probably added enough B-T-F.

The recommended usage of 12 ppm (parts per million) is the level used by many breweries <u>without a clean water rinse</u>. This level is attainable by using the cap of the 4 ounce bottle it comes in and adding two caps full of B-T-F to five gallons of water, or one cap full to 2 1/2 gallons of water. This is helpful if you believe your local water could be a source of bacteria and you think rinsing in such water would be likely to reinoculate harmful matter to your equipment, and especially to your homemade <u>wine or beer</u>. If your water quality is not a problem, you should rinse your equipment and containers as it can be helpful and reassuring, just in case you've been a bit heavy-handed with the sanitizer as we tend to be. Instructions for use come with B-T-F.

A sanitizing solution can also be made by adding 4 ounces of sodium bisulfite or potassium metabisulfite to 1 gallon of water, or 1 ounce to 1 quart of water. If you make this solution, add the bisulfite to a small amount of warm water and stir or shake the container until the bisulfite is completely dissolved. Then add the rest of the <u>cool</u> water. Try not to breathe the fumes of this mixture as it will have a pungent odor, and it can irritate your nose and lungs. After using this solution, rinse everything you sanitized with clean water.

If you run out of, or do not have the sanitizers we mention, a sanitizing solution can be made by adding <u>1 ounce</u> of unscented, liquid household bleach to <u>2 1/2 gallons of water</u>. If you use a bleach solution to sanitize your equipment, etc., be sure to rinse every- thing with clean water several times. You have to rinse several times to remove all traces of a bleach solution.

Caution:

When using chemicals for cleaning and or sanitizing, wear protective clothing, gloves and glasses.

Do not mix chemicals containing sulfite with any chemical containing chlorine (bleach) as they can produce dangerous chlo- rine gas.

Be sure to label and secure all cleaning and sanitizing chemicals where children can- not get to them.

VINEGARS UNLIMITED

Excellent wine vinegar can be made using <u>mother of vinegar,</u> <u>water and wine</u> as a base. The procedure for making vinegar is easy to follow and making your own home-made vinegar with mother is a very interesting do-it-yourself project. When you make your own vinegar, it is almost without limit as to the different kinds of vinegar you can make.

For instance, you can make apple cider vinegar from apple cider that has 6% to 12 % alcohol content. Apple cider vinegar is claimed by many people to be of great benefit to health and is also used externally for many things. Hardly a month goes by that we do not see an article on its various benefits.

(When making apple cider vinegar, we do not recommend the use of hard cider that has an alcohol content higher than 12%, or commercial hard cider that has been distilled.)

You can make your own apple cider (or apple wine) from fresh apples, or from commercially bottled 100 % apple juice that does not contain preservatives, additives, artificial flavor or coloring. In turn, when you make apple cider or apple wine, you can make your own vinegar.

You can make vinegar with nearly any kind of grape wine. You can also make your own vinegar with almost any fruit, berry or vegetable wine that has at least a 6% alcohol content. Whatever kind of vinegar you make is really a matter of choice. If you like one kind of vinegar, such as red burgundy wine vinegar, which happens to be one of our favorites, you can make it. You can also experiment by making small batches of vinegar, each made with a different kind of wine, and in the process, it is probable that you will come up with a gourmet vinegar that will be a real delight for you, your family and friends.

If you are a brewer of homemade beer,

you may want to try making a malt vinegar. When you make an all malt beer with at least 6% alcohol, save some of the wort (finished beer) in a wide mouth glass or food grade plastic container just before you bottle. Cover the container with a clean sanitized cloth and set the wort aside while you bottle your beer. Then add one part mother of vinegar (red or white) to three parts of the saved beer wort and let it work like wine vinegar, (see procedure pages 9 through 14). Then you can increase the amount with your next batch of all malt beer (6 % alcohol), by adding three parts of the finished beer to the malt vinegar you have working. (Example: if you have a quart of vinegar working, add three quarts of finished beer to it.) This should increase the malt flavor, and you could produce a malt vinegar you really enjoy.

Making vinegar with mother of vinegar can also be an educational project. When making vinegar in a wide mouth, one gallon glass jar you can view the process as the mother, water and wine convert to vinegar.

Homemade vinegar is usually made from wine containing 6% to 12% alcohol. During the process, as the mother converts

31

the wine to vinegar, the alcohol is converted to acetic acid. <u>Totally finished vinegar usually does not contain any alcohol</u>.

Among other reasons for making your own homemade vinegar, many commercially made vinegars (especially if they are distilled), in our opinion, have none of the exotic and stimulating flavors, aroma or quality of homemade vinegar.

Making vinegar could also become a profitable venture. There always seems to be a market for small production, gourmet wine vinegar. Should you become interested in producing your own vinegar as a commercial product, there are regulations and the sale of vinegar does require a license. You can get information on this by contacting your state food control or business license board.

MAKING GOOD HOMEMADE WINE

Making homemade wine and vinegar is becoming more popular each year, and you can set aside a portion of your homemade wine for making <u>your own vinegar;</u> many people do. Among the many benefits of making your own wine, you know how much sulfite (which at the time of this writing is usually necessary) has been added to the wine and if any additives, and how much, has been added to your wine.

Good homemade wine makes excellent homemade vinegar. Making your own homemade wine is an interesting pastime, and <u>we would like to recommend three inexpensive pieces of equipment</u> that when used, can be of great assistance to you in making good wine.

1) Hydrometer:

When making your own homemade wine, we strongly suggest that you use a 3 scale hydrometer. A hydrometer has a specific gravity scale, a potential alcohol scale, and a balling scale. Hydrometers are not expensive, and they can be used over and over again to help you eliminate potential problems.

A hydrometer is an essential tool when making wine and beer. Before the juice begins to ferment, a hydrometer will show you if your juice needs more, has enough, or has too much sugar.

The right amount of sugar in the juice is very important in the primary stage of fermenting your wine. Various fruits, berries, vegetables and grapes frequently do not contain enough natural sugar for proper fermentation. The addition of commercial sugar such as white cane sugar is usually necessary.

A hydrometer will also give you an estimate of the potential alcohol percentage of your finished wine. Then, when you make vinegar with your own homemade wine, you will know about how much water, if any, to add to the mother and wine.

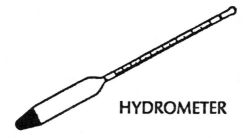

HYDROMETER

2) Acid Test Kit:

When making wine from grapes, berries, vegetables or fruits, it is often necessary to raise or lower the acid level of the juice before fermentation begins. If the acid level of the juice is too high, as it often is with grapes, gooseberries, elderberries, cherries and other fruit, (especially those grown in a northern climate), the finished wine may be too dry (biting or sharp) to your taste.

On the other hand, grapes grown in warm areas have a tendency to be low in acid; as do dates, raisins and figs. Among other things, low acid can produce an uninteresting wine and vinegar that will spoil easily.

Acid test kits are used for measuring total acidity of wine. Using an acid test kit will give you the necessary information and the opportunity to balance your wine (by using acid blend for example). Or to lower the total acidity level of the juice when too high. You can do this by diluting the juice with water, a little at a time before fermentation starts, then use your hydrometer and add sugar to bring the specific gravity up to the desired level. An acid test kit may be used before primary fermentation of the juice, during the fermentation process and for finished wine.

Acid test kits contain,
sodium hydroxide 0.100N (HaOH)
phenolphthalein (indicator)
flask, a 10 cc syringe and an eye dropper.
Instructions for use come with a kit.

3) Titret Kit:

If you add sulfites (potassium metabi-sulfite) to your wine during the winemaking process, as most winemakers do, a <u>Titret kit</u> is another kit that is recommended.

You can measure the level of sulfur dioxide (sulfite) in your homemade wine with the kit. This kit can be used at any stage of winemaking. This is especially important at bottling time if you think there may be too much sulfite in the wine, or if you are concerned about there not being enough.

The Titret kit can be of special interest if you use commercial wine for making your vinegar. You can open a bottle, jug or container of wine and test for the approximate amount of sulfite in the wine before using it to make your vinegar. As we said before, too much sulfite in the wine can destroy the mother.

A Word Of Caution:

It is not advisable to make a batch of homemade wine and vinegar from bottled wine at the same time. The reason, during the process the active vinegar spores from your vinegar may get into your batch of wine before it is bottled and degrade the wine.

However, should you throw caution out the door and decide to make your wine and vinegar at the same time, do not make or store them in the same building.

A person we met at a wine tasting did just that! He told us that he had had some vinegar working in the kitchen of his home. His wife wanted him to move it. Not thinking about the consequence, he moved the vinegar to his wine shed where he had over a hundred gallons of nearly finished wine. Unfortunately, vinegar spore invaded his unfinished wine and turned it into low grade vinegar.

Precaution: When making wine, you should not use any of the equipment that you use when making vinegar. However! If for whatever reason you do use the same equipment, be sure to <u>clean</u> and <u>sanitize</u> all the equipment before using it for making wine. Even after sanitizing there is a chance vinegar spore could get into your wine.

"Jim and George's Home Winemaking-- A Beginner's Book" has a chapter on the importance of using a hydrometer when making wine, and complete easy instructions for using one. The book also contains instructions on acid testing and information on sulfite testing.

Included in the book are complete easy instructions for making homemade wine. There are 25 recipes for berry, fruit and vegetable wines, and individual recipes for red grape wine and white grape wine.

Jim and George's Home Winemaking-- is an up-to-date, easy to read and easy to understand, home winemaking book written for the beginner.

NOTES ON MAKING GOOD HOMEMADE WINE

USING COMMERCIAL WINE
when making
HOMEMADE VINEGAR

We have made homemade vinegar with premium California wines, which was an expensive way to go but it made excellent vinegar. We have also made outstanding vinegar with commercial wine that is sold at markets in gallon bottles (commonly referred to as jug wine) and from 4 and 5 liter containers. Commercial wine bought in gallon bottles and 4 or 5 liter containers is usually the least expensive to use when making homemade vinegar.

We happen to live in the wine country of California, which is the main reason we have used commercially made California wine in making most of our vinegar. Having made small batches of vinegar with wine from many wineries, most of which produced fine to excellent vinegar, leads us to believe that most commercial wines made in California do not contain an excessive sulfite percentage. As we have said, excessive sulfite can destroy mother of vinegar. When in doubt about the amount of sulfite in commercial wine, a Titret kit can be used to determine the approximate amount.

When we are making vinegar with a commercial wine we have not tried before, we take a wee sample (sometimes more) for taste and aroma. If the taste and aroma are as good as we think they should be, we make a small batch of vinegar to see how it develops.

If it produces a gelatinous cap (mother) on the top, and when the vinegar is finished we like the taste, we make a larger batch. If it does not convert to vinegar or it does not have the taste we like, we add it to our "do not use for making vinegar" list. However in a couple of years or so you might want to try the same brand again, as by then the wine will probably be from another crop of grapes that has been crushed, fermented and bottled, and it may make great vinegar.

When testing different wines for making vinegar, we usually have about 3/4 of a gallon of red vinegar (mother) and the same amount of white vinegar (mother) working. By having both, we can test red or white wines to see if they will produce a vinegar to our liking. You can test several wines at the same time using a quart jar for testing each one. Using the proper amount of mother, water and wine, fill the jar or jars about 3/4 full. Cover the top of the jar with a sanitized cloth and let it work. When it is finished and you have used the taste test and you decide it will make a vinegar to your liking, you can pour the vinegar (which is mother) into a larger container. Add more water and wine to it and make a larger batch, and as you add more wine, the flavor of that wine will increase in the vinegar.

If you want to make vinegar with commercially made wine made in your area and you are unsure as to the sulfite content of the wine, as we said before you can use a Titret kit to determine the approximate amount of sulfite in any wine.

You can also make a small batch of

vinegar from the wine of your choice without testing for sulfite. Pour the amount of wine and water you are going to use into a container, stir and let it set for thirty minutes before you add the mother. This amount of time will allow some of the sulfite gas to escape. If in a few weeks the mixture forms a layer of mother on the top, which means it is working, and when you taste test it, it pleases your taste, make a larger batch.

NOTES ON COMMERCIAL WINE
variety tried, and result

SMALL QUANTITY OF VINEGAR

If you have a small amount of mother, say less than a half pint, a quart size canning jar will do as a starter. If you have a pint of mother, you can use up to a gallon size container.

When you start a batch of vinegar, we have suggested that you use <u>widemouth glass jars or widemouth food grade plastic containers</u>. If you use plastic containers, make sure they are <u>food grade</u>.

There are several reasons we use widemouth containers, instead of containers with small openings or necks, such as gallon jugs. Mother of vinegar forms a gelatinous layer on the top of the potential vinegar and a container with a small neck like a gallon jug

45

can make it difficult to draw off the finished vinegar, as the layer of mother often blocks the opening. Also, when cleaning the jug in preparation for a new batch of vinegar, it is somewhat difficult to remove the layer of mother. A bottle or container with a small neck also reduces the amount of air the culture needs, and the conversion to vinegar will be slower. The mixture of mother, water and wine, needs as much air as possible while converting to vinegar.

When using gallon size containers, look for widemouth gallon size glass jars or food grade plastic containers <u>with spigots</u> that can be removed for cleaning. Spigots make it easier to draw off the finished vinegar, and you draw off less sediment as you do not stir up the vinegar when using a spigot.

When you think your vinegar is finished and you are using a container without a spigot, you can remove and discard the layer of mother and dip or pour the amount of vinegar you need. Don't use all of it, leave some of the vinegar (which is mother) and pour it into a clean sanitized container, then add more water and wine, in the right proportions, to make more vinegar. A layer of mother will form on the top of the new batch.

Example of a half gallon and one gallon wide mouth jar.

When the jar is filled within about two inches of the top with mother, water and wine, cover with a piece of sanitized muslin or several layers of cheesecloth and tie with a string or secure the material to the top of the jar with a rubber band.

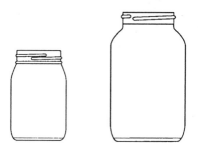

Homemade vinegar label

You can decorate a label with anything
that pleases you.

HOMEMADE
VINEGAR

TYPE

....

MADE BY ....

LARGER QUANTITY OF VINEGAR

After you have made a small batch of homemade vinegar or a few small batches with different kinds of wine, we are sure you will want to make a larger quantity. When bottled and labeled, homemade vinegars make great gifts for your family and friends especially during the holidays or on special occasions.

When you want to increase the amount of vinegar you are making and you have for example, a half gallon of finished vinegar (mother), you can add water and wine in the right proportion to your vinegar (see page 10). This will increase the amount of working vinegar (mother) to two gallons. For this amount of vinegar you will need 2 one gallon widemouth containers and a smaller widemouth container. Only fill each container a little over 3/4 full; this leaves enough space for the amount of air the mixture needs. Let the vinegar work for a few weeks, then you can add more water and wine in the right proportions and increase your total amount, according to your needs.

Let's say you want to make 4 gallons of vinegar. For this amount you will need about one gallon of <u>finished</u> vinegar (mother), and water and wine in the right proportion.

Example, mix about <u>one gallon</u> of finished vinegar (mother), with <u>one gallon</u> of water, and <u>two gallons</u> of wine that has 11% to 12% alcohol. If the percentage of alcohol in your wine is 9%, mix one gallon of vinegar, with 1/4 gallon of water and 2 and 3/4 gallons of wine. If your wine or apple cider (wine) is 6% alcohol, mix one gallon of vinegar with three gallons of wine.

Because you only fill each container a little over 3/4 full, you will need 5 one gallon wide mouth glass jars or food grade plastic containers. You can also make up to 5 gallons of vinegar, in a 6 gallon food grade plastic container <u>with a spigot</u>. A 6 gallon container takes less space than 5 one gallon containers, but weighs about forty-one pounds when full of vinegar, so store it where you will not have to move it. Keep in mind that you only fill each container a little over 3/4 full. Again, this is to allow enough air space for the vinegar to breathe.

If for whatever purpose you can use a larger quantity of vinegar, you can make your vinegar in 10, 20, or 32 gallon, food grade plastic containers with removable spigots. When you use plastic containers, make sure they are food grade containers. Containers that are not food grade can be harmful to your health.

Note:

Due to the acid content of vinegar, we do not use metal containers when making or storing homemade vinegar. We do not use crocks when making vinegar, wine or beer. Crocks are heavy and cumbersome and can have hairline cracks on the interior surface. If you decide to use a crock, check the interior surface for hair line cracks. Crocks with hairline cracks are difficult to sanitize.

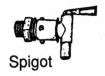
Spigot

6 Gal. bucket

10 Gal. container

20 Gal. container
w/dolly

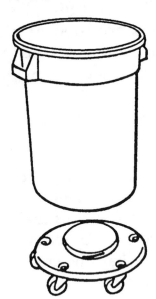
32 Gal. container
w/dolly

FILTERING YOUR VINEGAR

While drawing off your finished vinegar for use, the less you stir or disturb it the clearer it will be.   After you bottle and let it set for a time, any sediment that remains should settle to the bottom of the bottle as most homemade vinegar will clear on its own in time. If there is any sediment on the bottom of the bottle when you are ready to use it, pour slowly, most of the sediment will remain in the bottle.

However, if you believe your vinegar needs filtering, and you have a small batch, say up to a gallon, you can filter it through paper drip coffee filters, the basket type. (Insert the filter in the mouth of a jar and tie or rubber band it to the top.) If you have a few gallons, the vinegar can be filtered through a piece of clean, sanitized, preferably white muslin (sheeting) material or several layers of cheese cloth.

When making large batches of vinegar, the vinegar can be filtered with commercial filters. The type of filters shown can be used as gravity fed filters. The vinegar to be filtered must be located above the filter, and the receiving container below the filter.

CARTRIDGE FILTERS

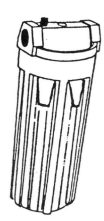

POLYPROPYLENE OR COTTON FIBER CARTRIDGES

NOTES ON FILTERING VINEGAR

PASTEURIZING YOUR VINEGAR

If you choose, you can pasteurize your filtered or non-filtered finished vinegar. Pasteurizing your vinegar will stop any further growth of the <u>mother of vinegar</u> and helps prevent spoilage of the vinegar when it is bottled and stored for a time.

Note:

Before you pasteurize your vinegar, be sure to draw off enough vinegar to start your <u>next batch</u>. (What you draw off is <u>mother of vinegar</u>.) Pasteurizing destroys the <u>mother,</u> and once pasteurized it will not produce vinegar. If you are not going to start more vinegar immediately, <u>the non-pasteurized mother</u> should be bottled. Use a bottle you can fill completely, and cap securely with a plastic cap or coated metal lid and store until you are ready to make more vinegar.

You may also want to draw off a pint or more of the non-pasteurized vinegar for immediate use. You can keep it in the refrigerator in a glass jar or bottle, capped securely with a plastic cap or coated metal lid.

Pasteurizing:

To pasteurize, heat the vinegar in a large pan for 30 minutes. (Do not use an aluminum pan unless coated, for example with a non stick material.) Heat at 150 degrees F. but not more than 160 degrees F. and test the temperature of the vinegar with a kitchen thermometer while heating. When the time is up, allow the vinegar to cool to about 70 degrees F. Use a sanitized dipper and a small funnel that will fit the neck of a bottle and dip your vinegar into clean sanitized rinsed bottles, then cap or cork the bottles securely.

Another way to pasteurize your vinegar is to pour it into clean, sanitized and rinsed bottles. If you are going to <u>cork</u> your bottles, leave enough space in each bottle for the cork. If you are going to <u>cap</u> the bottles, you can fill them to the top. Then place the <u>uncorked</u> or

<u>uncapped bottles</u> upright in a large pan and fill the pan with enough water to bring the water level up to just above where the necks of the bottles begin, and heat as above. Be careful; do not allow any of the water in the pan to get into the bottles. When finished heating, allow to cool to about 70 degrees F. then remove the bottles of vinegar from the pan and cork or cap the bottles securely.

If you have a large quantity of vinegar that has been <u>filtered</u>, pasteurized and cooled, you can siphon it into the bottles with a sanitized food grade siphon tube and a bottle filler that has an automatic shut off valve.

When pasteurized, bottled and corked or capped securely, your vinegar should keep for a long time, and when stored for about six months is usually very mellow. While aging, any sediment that may remain in the vinegar should fall to the bottom of the bottle. When you open a bottle or jar that has sediment on the bottom, you may want to pour the vinegar into another jar or bottle, and the slower you pour the less you will disturb the sediment.

Note: Do not put labels on the bottles until the bottles have been filled, corked or capped and wiped off to remove any vinegar on the outside of the bottle.

NOTES ON PASTEURIZING
and method used

FLAVORING YOUR VINEGAR WITH HERBS

Now that you have made your own vinegar, you might want to experiment and give some of the vinegar an additional flavor and or maximize the appearance of it when bottled.

You can do this by adding herbs that are used for human consumption and or cooking to your vinegar. Fresh herbs can add a slightly better flavor to vinegar, but either fresh or dried herbs can enhance your vinegar, and make it very tasty.

When using fresh herbs, the leaves and sprig can be used. They can be rinsed gently, damp dried and put into a bottle, then fill the bottle with vinegar. When using dried herbs, place the herbs in the vinegar and stir or shake gently to remove any air bubbles. Make sure the fresh or dried herbs are completely covered with vinegar by filling the bottle. Cap the bottle securely.

If you want to add herbs to your vinegar, fill one or several half pint bottles with vinegar and a small amount of a different herb in each bottle. Keep a record of the amount of herb you use. Fill the bottle(s), cap securely and let it age for about thirty days. Shake the bottle(s) occasionally.

When thirty days have passed, sample the vinegar for taste, if it has too much herb flavor, you can reduce the flavor by adding some of your regular vinegar. If it does not have enough flavor, you can add a little more herb; recap the bottle and let it age for a couple of weeks. There is no set amount of herbs to be added to vinegar so be sure to keep a record of the amount of herb you use with the amount of vinegar.

If you like the flavor a particular herb gives the vinegar, put it on your, "I like this herb vinegar" list. For any herb flavor you don't like, put it on your "don't care for" list, and try different herbs the next time.

Here are some flavoring herbs you may want to try: dill, thyme, tarragon, oregano, marjoram, basil, sage, rosemary, mustard seed, celery seed, mint, garlic, shallots and parsley or any other cooking herb. You can also combine herbs. For example a sprig of rosemary and a garlic clove, or chopped garlic makes a tasty combination. Be careful not to add too much garlic, as it can diminish the other flavors of the vinegar. Check the vinegar display at your local delicatessen or market for other combinations.

You can also add whole washed vegetables to your bottled vinegar to optimize the appearance. The only problem may be finding vegetables small enough to get into the neck of the bottle.

HOMEMADE
VINEGAR

NOTES ON FLAVORING
herb(s) used and amount of vinegar

ADDING OAK FLAVOR
to your vinegar

When you make or age vinegar in a barrel, the vinegar picks up some of the oak flavor of the barrel. When you make vinegar in containers other than barrels, you can add the oak flavor barrels give vinegar by adding a small amount of oak tea.

If you want to try it, boil a few clean, dried, aged, oak chips or oak shavings (the type that home wine and beermaking stores sell) in a cup of water for a few minutes to make an oak tea. (This oak tea is not for drinking.) It is only used for adding an oak flavor to your vinegar. Oak tea is also used to add an oak flavor to wine made in glass or plastic containers.

Allow the tea to cool, then strain out the oak pieces as you pour the tea it into a cup or jar and cover. When you are ready to use the tea, add a very small amount, <u>less than an eighth of a teaspoon</u>, to a cup of finished vinegar. Gently stir and taste. If you think the vinegar needs more oak flavor add a little more oak tea. Stir and taste again. Continue to add tea, and stir and taste until you get the flavor you want.

Don't add too much of the oak tea at a time, as you can over oak the flavor and dilute the flavor of your vinegar.

NOTES ON ADDING OAK FLAVOR
amount used, flavor obtained

BOTTLES, CORKS AND CAPS

The popular size bottle for bottling home made vinegar is the 375ml (milliliter) bottle. A 375ml bottle looks like a small wine bottle and is half the size of the standard 750ml wine bottle. Clear glass 375ml bottles are available at most home wine and beer-making supply stores in a cork style bottle for corking, or a screw top bottle for capping. The 375ml bottles with screw tops and plastic caps, often called sample bottles by winery people, are favored by those who don't want to cork their bottles.

If you choose to cork your bottles, you can use a "T" cork for corking the cork style bottle, instead of a standard wine cork. The advantage of using a "T" cork, which is a short cork that looks like a T, is that you do not need a corker to insert the cork into the bottle. The "T" cork has a beveled end and can be inserted into the bottle by hand. You can also re-cork the bottle easily with a "T" cork each time you use the vinegar. Off the subject; as part of our supplies we always take a few "T" corks with us on vacation to re-cork any wine bottles we may open.

If you want to use a standard wine cork # 9 x 1 3/4, it will also fit the 375ml bottle. However, if you use the standard cork, you will need a corker to insert the cork into the bottle.

When using corks, soak the corks in a solution of sodium bisulfite, or potassium metabisulfite (one ounce of bisulfite per quart of water) for about 20 minutes. This will sanitize the corks and soften them. You can then rinse the corks in clean water if you choose. Soaking the corks makes it easier to insert them into the bottles.

You can also store your vinegar in any bottle or jar that you can cork or cap securely. When you cap bottles or jars, use plastic caps or coated metal lids.

New bottles should be sanitized and

rinsed, and bottles you are reusing should be cleaned and sanitized just before using. Sanitize, rinse with clean water, and stand upside down to drain dry before filling. Caps and corks should also be sanitized at the same time.

Note:

It is not advisable to reuse standard wine corks. Once they have been used for corking a bottle and removed, they could contaminate the next bottle of vinegar or wine you cork. There is also the chance that used corks can leak, as corks can be damaged when being removed from a bottle with a cork puller.

"T" cork

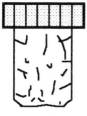

Standard cork

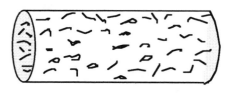

BOTTLE WASHER

BOTTLE BRUSH

WING STYLE CORKER

FLOOR CORKER

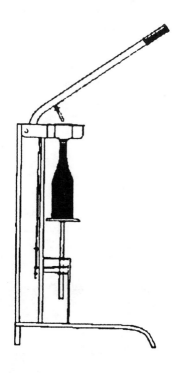

USABLE BOTTLES

375 milliliter bottles

type of bottles you get at the market

LABELS ENHANCE YOUR BOTTLED VINEGAR

When making homemade vinegar, many people make an extra amount to give to family members and friends, and or to enter at county fairs. You can bottle your vinegar, enhance the appearance, and give it a professional look by attaching a label to the bottle. If you have a little artistic ability, or you know someone who does, you can make your own labels, and attach them to the bottles using a glue stick. You can also buy commercial made labels.

The two labels illustrated on page 75 are dry gum (glue) back labels. Just dampen the back of the label with a wet sponge and place it on the bottle. For retail sale, labels are usually packaged 25 labels to a package.

Labels for bottled vinegar, wine and beer are available at home wine and beer-making supply stores.

HOMEMADE
VINEGAR

Made Especially
for Family & Friends

To _____

Made by _____

HOMEMADE
VINEGAR

Herbs

Made by _____

Homemade Herb Vinegar

Made by_____

Homemade

Zinfandel

Vinegar

Made by_____

MAKING VINEGAR IN A BARREL

A few generations ago a good vinegar barrel was a valued possession, particularly in rural communities. Today the interest in having a vinegar barrel is increasing as barrels not only produce great vinegar; they also make an interesting talking point and display.

Making vinegar in barrels is known as the Orleans method, and the procedure for making homemade vinegar (with mother of vinegar) in a barrel is the same as making vinegar in glass or food grade plastic containers. They are all considered the Orleans method.

Before you decide to make vinegar in a barrel, give some thought to it! Do you have a place where you can store a vinegar barrel and not have to move it? Depending on the size you choose, when you have added vinegar culture, water and wine to a barrel it can become quite heavy. Moreover, due to the shape of a barrel, it is awkward to handle.

A barrel should be stored above floor level on a strong stand, and the barrel should be placed in a barrel cradle or blocked to keep it from rolling. The barrel should also be high enough off the floor so that it is convenient to draw off vinegar with the spigot.

There should be unrestricted space over the top of the barrel. The space makes it convenient to add water and wine to the barrel with the funnel. Water and wine in the stated proportions should be added to the barrel each time you draw off vinegar for use. You can also add a little more water and wine than the vinegar you draw off, to make up for evaporation. You may also want a catch basin under the spigot, to catch any vinegar that is spilled.

If you decide you would like to have a vinegar barrel, the illustration on page 81 can be of help getting started.

The two air vent holes, (1 to 2 inch diameter holes according to the size of the barrel) one on each end of the barrel are necessary for air circulation, as your vinegar needs air during the conversion process from mother, water and wine to vinegar. The holes should be offset in height and covered with a fine non metal screen that will allow air circulation and keep insects out of your vinegar.

The spigot is also required; as it is the only way to get your vinegar out of the barrel.

The funnel is used when you add water and wine to the vinegar. The funnel should be food grade plastic and have a long neck. It can be supported in the bung hole with a silicon bung that has a hole large enough for the neck of the funnel. The long neck of the funnel extends below the layer of mother and almost to the bottom of the barrel to help mix the vinegar with water and wine when they are added to the barrel. The funnel is not removed, except when you clean the inside of the barrel. Several layers of cheese cloth can be placed in the mouth of the funnel to keep insects out when the funnel it is not being used.

Mother of vinegar forms a cap or layer of mother on the top of the vinegar and the layer continues to grow inside the barrel as long as there is air circulation. In time, the growing layer of mother could nearly fill the inside of a small barrel.

You can make your vinegar in a one or two gallon barrel, but we   that a three or five gallon barrel is a good size to use for a vinegar barrel. Barrels this size should produce enough vinegar for you and plenty to share with family and friends.

If you really get into making homemade vinegar in quantity, you can also make it in 10, 15, 20, or 30 gallon wine barrels.

Working Vinegar Barrel

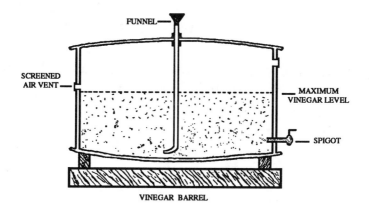

FUNNEL

SCREENED
AIR VENT

MAXIMUM
VINEGAR LEVEL

SPIGOT

VINEGAR BARREL

Storing vinegar in a barrel:

If you should decide to store and age your finished vinegar in a barrel, you will need a barrel that <u>does not</u> have air vent holes on each end. The barrel will have a bung hole on the side, and will need a hole for the spigot on one end. Keeping the bung in the bung hole should keep the barrel air tight, and when kept full of vinegar should reduce or stop growth of the mother.

When you draw off aged vinegar for use, it is best to replace the amount drawn off with fresh finished vinegar and keep the barrel topped off (full of vinegar).

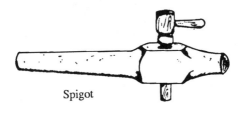

Spigot

Vinegar or Wine Storage Barrel

Storing wine in a barrel:

When you make homemade <u>wine</u> and if you decide to finish the fermentation and or store your wine in a barrel, a new barrel is a good choice. Follow the instructions that come with the barrel to prepare it for use, or you may want to try the method we have suggested on new barrel preparation. A new barrel must be prepared before it is used.

If you are thinking about using a barrel that has been used to store wine, try to find out if the wine that was stored in it turned to vinegar. Especially, don't use it for storing wine if the barrel has the smell of vinegar. Once vinegar has been in a barrel it is impossible for the home winemaker to destroy the vinegar spores. If you use a questionable barrel, there is a strong possibility your wine will turn into vinegar, or at the very least have an unpleasant odor and or taste. (Treatment of used barrels page 91.)

It is <u>not</u> advisable to store your wine in a barrel that has been used for something other than storing wine. (An example: used whiskey or brandy barrels are not recommended for storing wine or vinegar.)

NEW BARREL PREPARATION

A new barrel must be prepared for use before filling it with vinegar or wine and the process is called soaking or swelling the barrel. However, a barrel should not be soaked until you are ready to use it, as a barrel should be filled with vinegar or wine immediately after soaking. If it is not filled, it could dry out and leak.

When soaking or swelling a new barrel, the water you soak or swell it with is important. If your water is strongly chlorinated, use water that has been filtered to remove chlorine. If you cannot locate any filtered water, use a clean sanitized container and draw off the amount of water it will take to fill your barrel, stir vigorously and let it sit, covered with a clean sanitized muslin cloth or cheese cloth for twenty-four hours. Letting the water sit will allow some of the chlorine in the water to escape.

If your water contains a high content of iron and or sulfur, obtain the amount of water you need from a source that does not contain an excess amount of these elements. Iron and or sulfur residue in a barrel can create problems, such as iron haze and or unpleasant odors in your vinegar or wine.

Prior to soaking a barrel:

If you are going to use the barrel for making vinegar, drill and plug the air holes (1 to 2 inch diameter holes, according to the size of the barrel) on each end of the barrel and drill and plug the spigot hole (page 81). The spigot hole size is determined by the size spigot you are going to use. Spigots come in various sizes, from very small for one gallon barrels to large for thirty gallon barrels.

If you are going to store vinegar or wine in the barrel, the spigot hole is the only hole you drill and plug.

After drilling any holes, the barrel

should be rinsed to remove any wood chips and dust or other particles from inside the barrel. When the barrel is well rinsed inside and outside, make sure the barrel hoops are tight. Plug any drilled holes except the bung hole and <u>fill the barrel half to three quarters full of cold water.</u>

Soaking a barrel:

Caution: When soaking a barrel you use citric acid and potassium metabisulfite, **do not mix the two together** <u>before pouring into the barrel</u>. Mixing the two chemicals can create a gas that can irritate the eyes, nose and lungs.

Add <u>one level teaspoon</u> of <u>citric acid (dissolved in a little water)</u> for each gallon the barrel holds. Example: Add three level teaspoons to a 3 gallon barrel, or add five level teaspoons to a <u>five gallon barrel</u>.

Then, add one level <u>1/4 teaspoon of potassium metabisulfite</u> (completely dissolved in a small amount of water) for each gallon the <u>barrel holds</u>. Example: Add a level 3/4 teaspoon to a three gallon barrel, or add 1 & 1/4 level teaspoons to a five gallon barrel.

Fill the barrel with cold water, put the

bung in the bung hole securely, then roll the barrel back and forth several times, to mix the solution thoroughly.

It usually takes several days to a week, sometimes longer, to completely soak and swell a new barrel to the point where it will not leak. Remember to top off (fill) the barrel with water each day, as it will lose some water as it is swelling.

After the barrel has soaked for several days or more and it is not leaking, remove the bung and empty the barrel. When empty and drained, rinse the inside of the barrel several times.

Neutralize with citric acid:

Citric acid is used to neutralize any potassium metabisulfite that may remain in the barrel. Citric acid also has a sweetening effect on the barrel.

When you are sure the barrel is well rinsed, **fill** the barrel half to three quarters full of cold water.

Add <u>one level teaspoon</u> of <u>citric acid</u>

(<u>dissolved in a little water</u>) for each gallon the barrel holds. Example: Add three level teaspoons to a 3 gallon barrel, or add five level teaspoons to a <u>five gallon barrel</u>. Now roll the barrel back and forth several times to completely mix the solution.

When the solution is well mixed, **fill** the barrel (top off) with cold water and put the bung in the bung hole securely. Again, roll the barrel back and forth to mix the solution.

Let the barrel stand, full of the solution for 48 hours. At the end of 48 hours, empty the barrel and again rinse the inside of the barrel several times, drain, and be sure it is well drained.

Fill the barrel immediately:

If you are going to use the barrel for <u>making vinegar</u>, unplug the air holes in each end of the barrel and attach a fine <u>non</u> metal screen over the holes. Remove the plug from the spigot hole and insert the spigot. Insert a funnel with a long neck into the bung hole (see page 81). Fill the barrel to the bottom of the lower hole in one end of the barrel with the proper amount of mother, water and wine.

Or, as soon as you have rinsed and drained the barrel, and you are going to use it for storage, fill it with vinegar or wine, top off and insert the bung.

If your barrel should ooze a little of its contents, keep the outside of the barrel washed off to prevent mold from forming. If the barrel continues to leak, contact the people you bought it from, for ways to stop the leak or for a solution of the problem.

NOTES ON PREPARATION OF A NEW BARREL

TREATMENT FOR USED BARRELS

Due to the likely build up of chemical deposits (scale) inside wine barrels, and other reasons; wine barrels that have been used commercially or by unknown people for storing wine, etc, are not recommended for use by home vinegar or winemakers. (With the exception of when the barrel has been rebuilt and treated by a cooperage, barrel builder!)

Barrels that have been used to store whiskey or brandy are not recommended for use in making vinegar, or for storing vinegar or wine.

Keep in mind, regardless of how much you clean some used wine barrels; they may not be completely cleaned and sanitized. The vinegar, wine or even water you put in them, when drawn off for use may not be palatable or sanitary.

However, if you have bought or been given a used barrel, and you are determined to use it, <u>be sure you know what was in the barrel before you use it</u>. Remember, vinegar can be put in a barrel that has been used to store wine, but do not put wine in a barrel that has the smell of vinegar or that has been used to store vinegar.

Barrel preparation:

If you are going to use the barrel for <u>making</u> vinegar, drill the air holes in each end of the barrel (1 to 2 inch diameter according to the size of the barrel) and if it does not have one, a hole for the spigot, (page 81). (The size of the spigot hole is determined by the size spigot you are going to use.) Plug all the holes you drilled. but do not plug the bung hole.

If you are going to <u>store</u> vinegar or wine in the barrel, don't drill the air holes, just drill a hole for the spigot in one end of the barrel. See barrel illustration (page 83). Plug the spigot hole, but not the bung hole.

Barrel Cleaning:

There are several ways to attempt cleaning and sanitizing a used barrel. Check with your home wine and beermaking supply store for their suggestion, or you may want to try the following method.

Rinse the barrel several times to clean it and to remove any loose material. After you rinse it, make sure the hoops are tight and fill the barrel with cold water, put the bung in the bung hole and check the barrel to see if it leaks.

If it leaks, continue as you would for a new barrel. **Add** one level teaspoon of citric acid, dissolved in a little water for each gallon the barrel holds. Example: Add three level teaspoons to a 3 gallon barrel, or add five level teaspoons to a five gallon barrel. **Then**, add one level 1/4 teaspoon of potassium metabisulfite (completely dissolved in a small amount of water) for each gallon the barrel holds. Example: Add a level 3/4 teaspoon to a three gallon barrel, or add 1 & 1/4 level teaspoons to a five gallon barrel. It could take several days or more of soaking to stop leaks that may appear. Top off the barrel with water every day. **If the barrel does not leak or when leaks stop**, empty the barrel and rinse to remove any loose particles, then drain the barrel, and start the soda ash treatment.

Treatment with soda ash:

Cleaning a used barrel is essential. Soda ash (caustic soda) comes under the category of <u>caustic chemicals</u>, and it can be used to clean barrels and remove undesirable odor. It is also used in an effort to sanitize used barrels. Soda ash is <u>not recommended</u> for new barrels as it can leach out the oak flavor.

Caution: When you clean barrels with soda ash (caustic soda), a strong alkali and strong cleaner always wear gloves, protective clothing and eye protection.

Note: It is not recommended to use over 1/4 ounce of soda ash per gallon of water. Example: 3/4 ounce of soda ash to a three gallon barrel, or 1 and 1/4 ounce of soda ash to a five gallon barrel.

Once you have drained the barrel, fill it 1/2 to 3/4 full with <u>hot water</u>, 150 to 175 degrees F. and add <u>soda ash</u> (not over 1/4 ounce dissolved in a little water) per gallon of water the barrel holds when full. Add enough hot water to fill the barrel. Put the bung in the bung hole, <u>but not tight</u>, and roll the barrel back and forth to mix the solution. Let the solution remain in the barrel for at least 24 hours and roll the barrel back and forth occasionally to help loosen any scale that may be in the barrel. Then empty and rinse the inside of the barrel a number of times with cold water. If you continue to get scale out of the barrel when you rinse, you may have to repeat the soda ash treatment.

When you believe the inside of the barrel is as clean as you can get it and well rinsed, it is time to <u>add citric acid</u> as a neutralizer. Fill the barrel 1/2 to 3/4 full of hot water (150 to 175 degrees F). Dissolve the citric acid in a little water and **add** <u>one level teaspoon</u> of <u>citric acid</u> for each gallon of liquid the barrel holds. Example: Add three level teaspoons to a 3 gallon barrel, or add five level teaspoons to a five gallon barrel. Insert the bung in the bung hole and rock the barrel back and forth to mix the solution.

Now fill the barrel completely with hot

water, insert the bung <u>loosely</u> into the bung hole, (if you put it in tight you may have a problem removing the bung when the water cools) again, rock the barrel back and forth to mix the solution. Let the barrel stand for 24 hours, and rock it back and forth occasionally. After 24 hours empty the barrel, rinse it several times with cold water and drain well.

At this point we must repeat: No matter how much the home vinegar or winemaker cleans some used wine barrels, they may not be cleaned and sanitized completely. The vinegar or wine you put in them, when drawn off may not be palatable and or sanitary.

Using the barrel:

If you are going to use the barrel for <u>making vinegar</u>, unplug the air holes in each end of the barrel and attach a fine <u>non</u> metal screen over the holes. Remove the plug from the spigot hole and insert the spigot.

Insert a funnel that has a long neck into the bung hole (see page 81). Fill the barrel with the proper amount of mother, water and wine, to the bottom of the lower hole in one end of the barrel.

When you are using the barrel <u>for stor-</u><u>age</u> of vinegar or wine (see illustration page 83), remove the plug from the spigot hole and insert the spigot. Fill the barrel with vinegar or wine, top off and insert the bung in the bung hole. If the wine is still fermenting, insert an airlock and bung in the bung hole.

Your barrel may ooze a little of its cont-ents, if it does, keep the outside of the barrel washed off to prevent mold from forming. If the barrel continues to leak, contact a home wine and beermaking supply store for ways to correct the problem.

If you empty a barrel after using it, and you are going to leave it empty for a time, see (Page 99) for a way to keep it from drying out.

NOTES ON PREPARATION AND CLEANING OF A USED BARREL
and method used

CARE OF EMPTY BARREL

When you have used a barrel for storing wine or vinegar and it has been drained, it should not be left empty as it can dry out. One way to overcome this problem is to use cold water and rinse the barrel several times. Then fill it about 3/4 full of cold water. Add citric acid and potassium metabisulfite solution (see **soaking a barre**l, page 87 for amounts) and roll the barrel from side to side to mix. Fill the barrel with cold water and put the bung in the bung hole tightly. Check the water level every two or three weeks and add water if needed. Change the water, potassium metabisulfite and citric acid solution every two or three months. Check the barrel frequently for mold and odor.

When you are ready to use the barrel again, drain it and rinse several times. Then, once again follow the instruction to <u>neutralize with citric acid</u>.

Neutralize with citric acid:

Citric acid is used to neutralize any potassium metabisulfite that may remain in the barrel. Citric acid also has a sweetening effect on the barrel.

When you are sure the barrel is well rinsed, **fill** the barrel half to three quarters full of cold water.

Add <u>one level teaspoon</u> of <u>citric acid (dissolved in a little water)</u> for each gallon the barrel holds. Example: Add three level teaspoons to a 3 gallon barrel, or add five level teaspoons to a <u>five gallon barrel</u>. Now roll the barrel back and forth several times to completely mix the solution.

When the solution is well mixed, **fill** the barrel (top off) with cold water and put the bung in the bung hole securely. Again, roll the barrel back and forth to mix the solution.

Let the barrel stand, full of the solution for 48 hours. At the end of 48 hours, empty the barrel and again rinse the inside of the barrel several times, drain, and be sure it is well drained.

When the barrel has been neutralized, drained, rinsed and drained again, fill the barrel with vinegar or wine immediately.

CONVERSION TABLE

1 Gallon = 4 quarts = 8 pints = 128 ounces

1 Quart = 2 pints = 4 cups = 32 ounces

1 Pint = 2 cups = 16 ounces

1 Cup = 8 ounces

1 Pound = 16 ounces

1/2 Pound = 8 ounces

1/4 Pound = 4 ounces

1/8 pound = 2 ounces

1 Fluid ounce = 2 tablespoons = 6 teaspoons

1/2 Fluid ounce = 1 tablespoon = 3 teaspoons

3 Fluid Teaspoons = 1 tablespoon

1/2 of 1/4 Fluid Teaspoon = 1/8 teaspoon

CONVERSION COMPONENT

To convert from	To	Multiply by
Cups	Ounces	8.0
Gallons	Liters	3.79
Grams	Milligrams	1000
Grams	Ounces	0.035
Kilograms	Grams	1000
Kilograms	Ounces	35.27
Kilograms	Pounds	2.2
Liters	Gallons	0.264
Liters	Ounces	33.8
Liters	Pints	2.11
Liters	Quarts	1.06
Ounces	Grams	28.3
Pints	Gallon	0.125
Pints	Ounces	16
Pounds	Grams	453.6
Quarts	Liters	0.946
Tablespoons	Ounces	0.5
Tablespoons	Milliliters	15
Teaspoons	Milliliters	5
Teaspoons	Tablespoons	3

INDEX

WHERE TO OBTAIN
MOTHER OF VINEGAR AND EQUIP-
MENT

You can use any equipment or items of your own, that are similar to the items suggested in this book. For any items you do not have, they are available at:

Home Wine and Beermaking supply stores

Look in the yellow pages of your phone book, or that of a large city nearby for a listing, or call information.

If you cannot locate a home wine and beermaking supply store in your vicinity, write to: **A - Publishing**. We will refer your letter to a home wine and beermaking supply

store that will send you a catalog. The catalog will contain the items you need, including
<u>Mother of Vinegar</u> and home wine and beer-
making supplies.

A- Publishing
Post Office Box 5523 Napa, CA 94581
Telephone (707) 255-6408

Make and Enjoy Your Own Wine:

Jim and George's Home Winemaking
A Beginner's Book

Jim and George's home winemaking is
an excellent source book when making your
own fruit and grape wine. The 1995 edition of
the book has been revised and updated. The
book is written for beginner's who would like
to make their own wine, without getting
into the technical side of winemaking.

The book is easy to read and practical.
It contains information and complete instructions for making one, three or five gallons of
fruit, flower or vegetable wines from twenty-
seven recipes. Included are recipes and
instructions for making white grape wine and
red grape wine.

See order form page 110.

ORDER FORM

A - Publishing
Post Office Box 5523
Napa, CA 94581 / or call (707) 255-6408

Please send me the following books:

_____ Jim and George's Home winemaking
A Beginner's Book   by Jim Weathers $ 6.95 each.
second edition, 1995

_____ Homemade Wine Vinegar / made with
Mother of Vinegar $ 6.95 each.
by Pat and Carole Watkins, 1995

Sub Total_____

Calif. Residents please add sales tax-------------------

Shipping_____

Total_____

Name:_____

Address:_____

City:_____State:_____Zip:_____

Shipping:
$ 2.25 for first book, .75 cents for each additional book.

_____ I do not want to wait 3-4 weeks for my book(s) sent
book rate. I have included $ 3.50 per book for first
class mail.
Prices subject to change.

ORDER FORM

A - Publishing
Post Office Box 5523
Napa, CA 94581 / or call (707) 255-6408

Please send me the following books:

_____ Jim and George's Home winemaking
A Beginner's Book   by Jim Weathers $ 6.95 each.
second edition, 1995

_____ Homemade Wine Vinegar / made with
Mother of Vinegar $ 6.95 each.
by Pat and Carole Watkins, 1995

Sub Total_____

Calif. Residents please add sales tax-------------------

Shipping_____

Total_____

Name:_____

Address:_____

City:_____State:_____Zip:_____

Shipping:
$ 2.25 for first book, .75 cents for each additional book.

_____ I do not want to wait 3-4 weeks for my book(s) sent
book rate. I have included $ 3.50 per book for first
class mail.

Prices subject to change.